✳ Smithsonian

LITTLE EXPLORER

INVERTEBRATES

A 4D BOOK

by Melissa Ferguson

PEBBLE
a capstone imprint

Download the Capstone **4D** app!

- Ask an adult to download the Capstone 4D app.
- Scan the cover and stars inside the book for additional content.

When you scan a spread, you'll find fun extra stuff to go with this book! You can also find these things on the web at www.capstone4D.com using the password: invertebrates.26455

Smithsonian Little Explorer is published by Pebble,
1710 Roe Crest Drive, North Mankato, Minnesota 56003
www.mycapstone.com

Library of Congress Cataloging-in-Publication Data
Names: Ferguson, Melissa, author.
Title: Invertebrates : a 4D book / by Melissa Ferguson.
Description: North Mankato, Minnesota : an imprint of Pebble,
[2019] | Series: Smithsonian little explorer. Little zoologist |
Audience: Age 4–8. Identifiers: LCCN 2018004126 (print) |
LCCN 2018009131 (ebook) | ISBN 9781543526578 (eBook PDF)
| ISBN 9781543526455 (hardcover) | ISBN 9781543526516
(paperback) Subjects: LCSH: Invertebrates—Juvenile literature.
Classification: LCC QL362.4 (ebook) | LCC QL362.4 .F47 2019
(print) | DDC 592—dc23
LC record available at https://lccn.loc.gov/2018004126

Editorial Credits

Michelle Hasselius, editor; Kazuko Collins, designer;
Svetlana Zhurkin and Morgan Walters, media researchers;
Kris Wilfahrt, production specialist

Our very special thanks to Jen Zoon, communications specialist at
Smithsonian's National Zoo, for her review. Capstone would also
like to thank Kealy Gordon, Product Development Manager, and
the following at Smithsonian Enterprises: Ellen Nanney, Licensing
Manager; Brigid Ferraro, Vice President, Education and Consumer
Products; and Carol LeBlanc, Senior Vice President, Education and
Consumer Products.

Image Credits
Alamy: Natural History Collection, 13 (top); AP Images: Daily News-
Record/Nikki Fox, 5 (top); Getty Images: Aaron Ferster, 4, Reinhard
Dirscherl, 15; iStockphoto: kevdog818, cover; Minden Pictures: Fred
Bavendam, 7, Pete Oxford, 8; Newscom: imageBROKER/Helmut
Corneli, 28, Splash News/Jeff Moore, 16; Shutterstock: Antonio
Martin, 20, Arto Hakola, 24, Audrey Snider-Bell, 9, bluehand, 10,
Cathy Keifern, 13 (bottom), Cheryl Thomas, 12, David Litman, 21,
DavidNNP, 5 (bottom), Gerald Robert Fischer, 1, Kjersti Joergensen,
14, Nonthawit Doungsodsri, 11, Norhayati, 29, pr2is, 6, Salparadis,
19, Sergio Sallovitz, 18, Steve Bower, 25, Taras Chykhman, 2;
Smithsonian's National Zoo: Abby Wood, 17, 29, Mehgan Murphy, 22,
23, 27, Photo courtesy of Connor Mallon, 26

Design Elements by Shutterstock

Printed and bound in the United States.
PA021

TABLE OF CONTENTS

INVERTEBRATES AT THE ZOO

The Smithsonian's National Zoo is home to 1,800 animals from around the world. Invertebrates are a class of animals. They come in many shapes, sizes, and colors. Some live on land. Others call the ocean their home. All invertebrates have one thing in common—they do not have backbones.

YOU CAN BE A ZOOLOGIST!

Zoologists have an exciting job. They study the behaviors of animals in a zoo. To become a zoologist, you have to go to college and study hard. Then you can work with animals every day too.

More than 90 percent of the world's animals are invertebrates.

You can find Smithsonian's National Zoo in Washington, D.C. The Zoo was started in 1889. More than 2 million people visit each year. The Smithsonian Conservation Biology Institute (SCBI) was founded in 1974. SCBI scientists study ways to help protect and save endangered animals.

GIANT PACIFIC OCTOPUS

The giant Pacific octopus is the largest species of octopus on Earth. It's 10 to 25 feet (3 to 7.6 meters) long. It weighs between 22 and 400 pounds (10 to 181 kilograms). The octopus lives in the Northern Pacific Ocean. It eats shrimp, lobsters, and small sharks.

The biggest giant Pacific octopus ever recorded weighed more than 400 pounds (181 kg).

The giant Pacific octopus is one smart invertebrate. It can figure out how to get through mazes and can even recognize faces.

Because of its soft body, the giant Pacific octopus can squeeze into small spaces and under rocks. If a predator gets too close, the octopus squirts a cloud of ink to get away. It can also change color to blend in with its surroundings.

GOLIATH BIRD-EATING TARANTULA

Goliath bird-eating tarantulas are no ordinary spiders. They are some of the world's largest tarantulas. Their legs span 11 inches (28 centimeters). That's about the size of a dinner plate!

Despite their name, goliath bird-eating tarantulas rarely eats birds.

Goliath bird-eating tarantulas give a special warning to animals who get too close. They rub the hairs on their legs together, creating hissing noises. The sound can be heard 15 feet (4.6 m) away.

Goliath bird-eating tarantulas live in the rain forests of northern South America. They are active at night and rest during the day. In the wild they eat mice, frogs, lizards, and other invertebrates. The Smithsonian's National Zoo has two goliath bird-eating tarantulas. Keepers feed them cockroaches at the Amazonia exhibit.

NAUTILUS

What animal species was on Earth before the dinosaurs? The nautilus. The sea creature is called a living fossil. It looks the same as it did 400 million years ago.

The USS *Nautilus* was named after the sea animal. It was the world's first nuclear-powered submarine.

Some people hunt the nautilus for its unique shell.

The nautilus can be found near coral reefs in the Indian Ocean and Pacific Ocean. It is a cephalopod, like the octopus and squid. The nautilus' tentacles are attached to its head. It has more than 90 tentacles, which it uses to grab prey. The nautilus eats fish, crabs, and shrimp.

The nautilus has an outer shell that protects its soft body. The shell has different chambers that help the animal float in the water.

MONARCH BUTTERFLY

Monarch butterflies are known for their bold orange and black wings. Their bright colors serve an important purpose. They warn predators that the butterflies are toxic if eaten.

THE MIGRATION ROUTE OF THE MONARCH BUTTERFLY

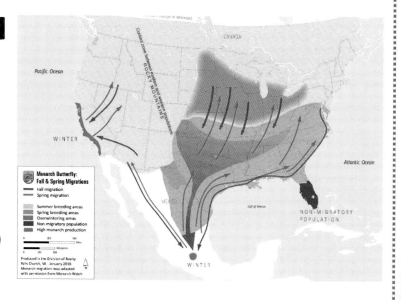

Monarch butterflies can travel between 50 and 100 miles (80 and 161 kilometers) a day.

Each year in the fall, monarch butterflies in Eastern North America fly to Mexico, where it's warmer. Monarch butterflies in Western North America travel to California for the winter. They return home in the spring.

Monarch caterpillars only eat leaves from the milkweed plant. The milkweed has a toxic chemical that helps protect the caterpillars from being eaten by other animals.

PEACOCK MANTIS SHRIMP

Peacock mantis shrimp can hit predators with lightning speed. Scientists believe they can strike as fast as a .22 caliber bullet. Their claws are strong enough to break glass. Peacock mantis shrimp also have amazing eyesight. These animals can see 10 times as many colors as humans.

Scientists are working on a camera that copies the vision of peacock mantis shrimp. They hope to use the camera to detect cancers in humans.

The multicolored shell of a peacock mantis shrimp can be bright blue, green, red, or orange. Its forearms are covered in spots.

Peacock mantis shrimp are crustaceans. They live in the Indian and Pacific Oceans. The shrimp make their homes in the grooves of coral and under rocks. Peacock mantis shrimp feed on crabs and mollusks.

GOLDEN SILK ORB-WEAVER SPIDER

Golden silk orb-weaver spiders are known for spinning webs made of golden silk. Insects, small birds, and other creatures that get caught in the webs become food for the spiders. Their webs can reach 3 feet (0.9 m) in length. Only female golden silk orb-weavers build webs. They are larger and more powerful than the male spiders. Females are 1 to 2 inches (2.5 and 5 cm) long.

Golden silk orb-weaver spiders live in warm climates. They can be found in Australia.

In 2012 a cape made from golden orb-weaver silk was on display at the Victoria and Albert Museum in London.

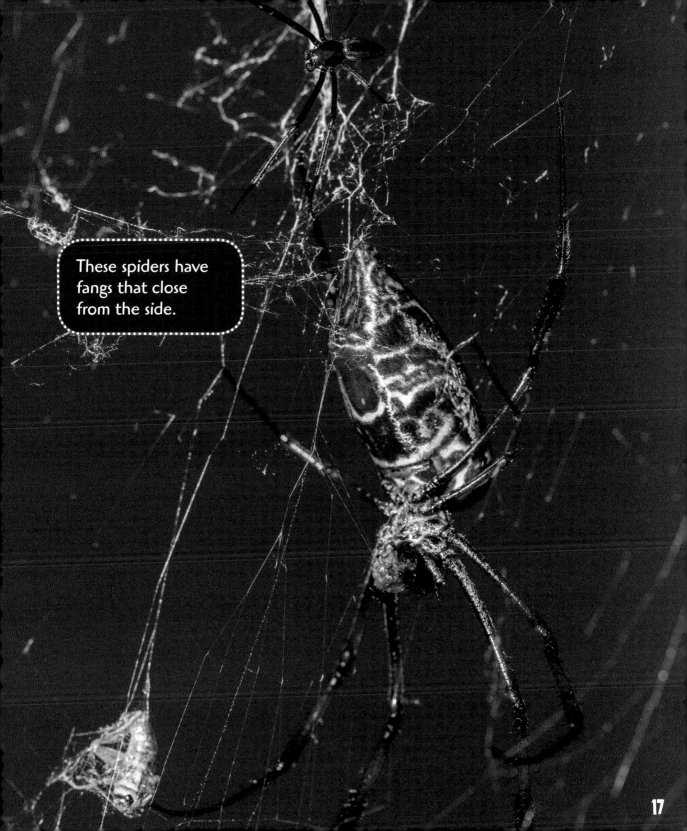

These spiders have fangs that close from the side.

⭐ LEAF-CUTTER ANT

Leaf-cutter ants live in huge colonies in the rain forests of South and Central America. Like other ant species, each ant in the colony has a job to do. Soldier ants protect the queen. Other ants are workers. Worker ants don't have wings. Smaller worker ants are called minima workers. They work on the inner parts of the colony.

In a colony, only the queen is able to have offspring.

A leaf-cutter ant colony can contain millions of ants.

Leaf-cutter ants use their strong jaws to cut leaves from trees. Then they carry the leaves back to their nests. The leaves are used to grow fungus. The ants eat the fungus. Because they grow their own food, leaf-cutter ants are known as the farmers of the insect world.

TUBE ANEMONE

Tube anemones are found in the Mediterranean Sea. They are 15.7 inches (40 cm) long. Their soft bodies are covered by tubes. If tube anemones sense danger, they can hide inside their tubes.

Tube anemones can live for 50 years or more.

Tube anemones are brightly colored. They can be tan, pink, purple, or even fluorescent green.

Tube anemones are carnivores. This means they eat other animals, including small fish and shrimp. They have two sets of tentacles. Tube anemones use their outer tentacles to catch prey. They use their inner tentacles to move prey into their mouths.

GIANT CLAM

Giant clams live in shallow water in the Pacific Ocean. These clams are the largest mollusks in the world. Their shells are more than 4 feet (1.3 m) long. They can weigh more than 500 pounds (227 kg).

Giant clams are omnivores. This means they eat both plants and animals. Giant clams mainly eat sugar and protein made by algae that live in the clams' tissues.

In 2006 a fisherman found a 75-pound (34-kg) pearl inside a giant clam in the Philippines. He kept the pearl under his bed as a good luck charm for 10 years. The pearl is believed to be worth at least $100 million.

EASTERN LUBBER GRASSHOPPER

The word *lubber* means big and clumsy. It's a fitting name for these grasshoppers. Eastern lubber grasshoppers have wings, but they can't fly. Instead, the insects walk and make short, awkward hops.

If lubber grasshoppers are threatened, they'll release a stinky, foamy spray.

Lubber grasshoppers are some of the largest grasshoppers. They can grow up to 3 inches (7.6 cm) long.

Eastern lubber grasshoppers live in the southeastern United States. Like monarch butterflies, their bright colors warn predators to stay away. They are toxic if eaten. These grasshoppers eat leaves and plants.

ELEGANCE CORAL

Elegance coral have green and pink-tipped tentacles. They can be found in the Indian and Pacific Oceans. Visitors to the Smithsonian's National Zoo can see an elegance coral at the Coral Lab exhibit in Amazonia.

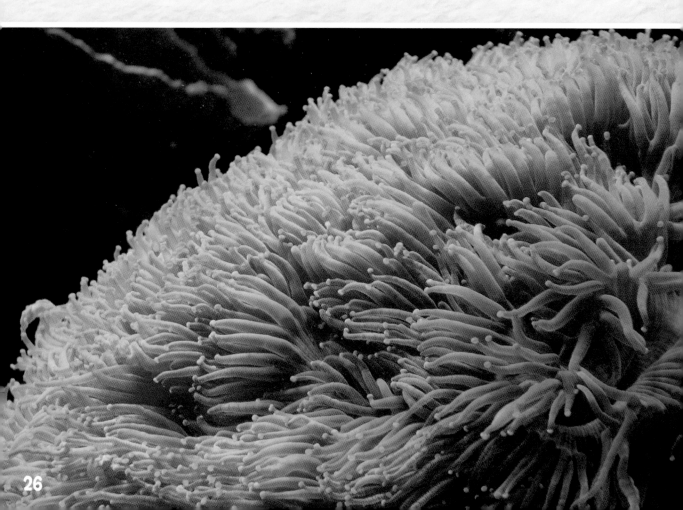

Like many coral species across the world, elegance coral are threatened by humans. Coral are used to decorate aquariums and make jewelry. In the ocean, coral are exposed to warmer temperatures due to the changing climate. The Smithsonian Conservation Biology Institute is working to protect these coral and coral reefs.

ELKHORN CORAL

Elkhorn coral are recognized by their many thick branches. The branches look like elk antlers. Elkhorn coral are used as habitats for small animals, including shrimp, fish, and lobsters. The coral can be found in shallow water in Florida and the Caribbean.

Elkhorn coral can grow to 6.6 feet (2 m) tall.

Elkhorn coral was one of the first coral species to be protected under the Endangered Species Act of 1973. This act protects animals that are endangered or threatened.

Like elegance coral, elkhorn coral are damaged by the changing climate. When ocean temperatures rise, the algae inside the tissues leave. The coral turn white. This is called bleaching. Coral bleaching kills most coral.

GLOSSARY

algae—small plants without roots or stems

backbone—a set of connected bones that run down the middle of the back

cephalopod—a group of ocean-dwelling mollusks, including the octopus and squid

chamber—an enclosed space within an animal's body

climate—the usual weather that occurs in a place

colony—group of animals that live closely together

coral reef—a structure made up of the hardened bodies of corals

crustacean—a sea animal with an outer skeleton, such as a crab, lobster of shrimp

endangered—in danger of dying out

fluorescent—glowing in color

fungus—a living thing similar to a plant, but without flowers or leaves

habitat—the natural place and conditions in which a plant or animal lives

migration—the regular movement of animals as they search different places for food

mollusk—a soft-bodied creature that usually has a shell

predator—an animal that hunts other animals for food

prey—an animal hunted by another animal for food

shallow—an area of water that is not very deep

species—a group of plants or animals that have the same ancestor and share common characteristics

tentacle—a long armlike body part some animals use to move, touch, feel, and grab

toxic—poisonous

CRITICAL THINKING QUESTIONS

1. What are invertebrates? How are they different from vertebrates?

2. Tiny leaf-cutter ants called minima workers do jobs inside the ant colony. What are maxima workers? What is their job in the colony?

3. Elkhorn coral are protected under the Endangered Species Act. Name another invertebrate that is protected under this act.

READ MORE

Knight, P.V. *Bird-Eating Spiders.* Spiders, Eight-Legged Terrors. New York: Gareth Stevens Publishing, 2018.

Moore, Heidi. *Giant Tube Worms and Other Interesting Invertebrates.* Creatures of the Deep. Chicago: Raintree, 2012.

Young, Karen Romano. *No Bones!* Penguin Young Readers. New York: Penguin Young Readers, 2016.

INTERNET SITES

Use FactHound to find Internet sites related to this book.

Visit www.facthound.com

Just type in 9781543526455 and go.

 **Super-cool stuff!** Check out projects, games and lots more at **www.capstonekids.com**

INDEX